KON IN SPRINGTIME

TONY CONNOR

KON IN SPRINGTIME

POEMS

LONDON
OXFORD UNIVERSITY PRESS
NEW YORK   TORONTO

Oxford University Press, Ely House, London W.1

GLASGOW NEW YORK TORONTO MELBOURNE WELLINGTON
CAPE TOWN SALISBURY IBADAN NAIROBI DAR ES SALAAM LUSAKA ADDIS ABABA
BOMBAY CALCUTTA MADRAS KARACHI LAHORE DACCA
KUALA LUMPUR SINGAPORE HONG KONG TOKYO

First Published 1968
Reprinted 1970

PRINTED IN GREAT BRITAIN

FOR
KONSTANTIN SOLOWIENSKI

ACKNOWLEDGEMENTS

ACKNOWLEDGEMENTS are due to the Editors of the following periodicals in which some of these poems have previously appeared: *Ambit, Continuum, The Critical Quarterly, Consumption, Granta, The Malahat Review, Manifesto,* and *Massachusetts Review.* An earlier version of 'Twelve Secret Poems' appeared in the series of poetry pamplets isssued by the Manchester Institute of Contemporary Arts.

CONTENTS

An Absence   1
A Child Half-Asleep   4
The Nestling   5
A Child Picking its Nose   6
Children's Games   7
Inheritors   8
In the Children's Room   9
Manhood and Youth   10
Saying It   11
Cavalry Sketches   12
Flights
    for Edward Weismiller   18
Druid's Circle   20
On the Campus   21
Approaching Bolton   22
Above Penmaenmawr   24
On the Cliff   25
Considering Junk   27
My Sister's Papers   28
The Globe Inn   29
The Gamekeeper's Dotage   31
Kon in Springtime   32
The Bat, the Rat, the Stench, the Locked-Out God   34
Twelve Secret Poems   38

vii

AN ABSENCE

ALONE in the house, trying to write,
I read, wander about, eat fruit.

The kitchen's a mess; my wife has left
a pile of dishes. I shall not shift

a single one, but shall take care
to wash what I use; the rest can stay there

until she returns. I yawn, I grieve,
wanting her back and hating love.

Were she to walk in now I'd sulk
about those dishes, or spilt talc,

or something else. In bed my danger
would be apparent, like that of a stranger

who'd charmed a girl to a quick fuck.
Afterwards I'd relax and talk.

But here I am, alone for at least
a week more. I must make the best

of silence; still my mind, my heart
to a single peace, then harvest it.

*

I fidget, shift my legs. An itch
has got the top of my back; I stretch

an arm behind to find the spots
which she says are red as beetroots.

I

They need attention. She squeezes
them every week; I think it pleases

her more than she will care to admit—
to do me good, and also hurt.

She tells me all my handsome acts
have disfigured, blackheaded backs,

after their father. She says with relish
her duties do not end at flesh,

but reach into my noblest daydreams;
I think she would like to write my poems.

*

And there I have her. While she's gone
I'll write a sequence about The Engine:

banjo unions, gear-teeth, sumps—
allusions she won't as much as glimpse

the meaning of. I'll keep my pride
with allegories of the axle-rod,

the crank-shaft bearings, the differential—
things she doesn't understand at all.

*

Now I've recovered. I feel better,
and I might write her a brief letter

explaining my plan. She will conclude
I intend her to become annoyed

2

and will write back sweetly, with a vague hint
that maybe, possibly, she is pregnant.

And I shall finger my spots, and sit;
unable even to masturbate.

A CHILD HALF-ASLEEP

STEALTHILY parting the small-hours silence,
a hardly-embodied figment of his brain
comes down to sit with me
as I work late.
Flat-footed, as though his legs and feet
were still asleep.

On a stool,
staring into the fire,
his dummy dangling.

Fire ignites the small coals of his eyes;
it stares back through the holes
into his head, into the darkness.

I ask what woke him?

'A wolf dreamed me.' he says.

THE NESTLING

A DEAD bird
in a polythene bag

all day from hot
hand to hot hand

fumbled through
the crinkly window.

Gawping close faces
bright eyes at the eyelid

closed for ever,
brains eating death.

By evening maggots,
a bagful

ghosts of worms
troubling the still world

of the sealed coffin
I toss in the dustbin

with the sentimental
disgust of the dying.

A CHILD PICKING ITS NOSE

He is absorbed; bright eyes fixed on infinity—
a poet trying to get the poem out.
At the end, his laughter is a shout;
the crow's on his nail; he offers it to me.

CHILDREN'S GAMES

Papu, Tariq, Oguchi, Paulo,
screeching and bawling various Englishes
beneath the blizzarding wind-rocked hawthorn
next to my air-raid shelter.

Who told you I love you?

The Catholic merchant grinds his ghost's teeth
where your parents divide his house;
your teacher laments his choice of trade;
the shopkeepers can hardly bear
pocketing your families' income.

But play by my notoriously public tree.
The dogs have stunk it,
the neighbours have lopped its symmetry,
the authorities have declared it unsafe,
and though I do not love you

if you fight
friendly with my infants
they might.

Play while the sickly-scented snow
tumbling on your tumblings
is all you need know.

Play while your parents divide England.

INHERITORS

They drift and streak
at the corner of the eye.
They pull the mind sideways
until it is a long thin thing
that twangs back
scattering thoughts.

They gather everything
into a podgy sticky parody
of masterful age
whose compact tons
are everywhere you look
and cannot be stepped round.

They will journey from the ends of the earth
to attend your funeral
when eventually you trip over them
and break your neck.

IN THE CHILDREN'S ROOM

SOMETIMES when they are asleep,
I stand by the beds looking
at those beautiful variations
of the sadly drooping
flesh on our bones. I long,
on such nights, for mastery

of their futures; as though they
might benefit by magic
of my close care—protected
from the poison and decay
of time, and the stains that mock
clean intention. But the dead,

who haunt my house severely,
raise their loud voices against
such nonsense, and I think of
my own poems: how slowly,
and from what fallings and stains
they have grown; likewise my love.

Then I bend, and smooth-back hair
from a hot forehead, or, maybe,
stroke a cheek. Not reconciled
to the undoubted wearing-
out and dirtying they
must suffer to die wise men,

or fools; but less troubled by
the futility of my fierce
prayers, and the proud but modest
gestures of fatherly
love I make as though by force
of habit over each bed.

MANHOOD AND YOUTH

WHEN first the lean-flanked, cold-eyed Goddess
entered my bed, she wore the hazy face

of nameless women, hardly known, remembered
from crowded city streets, or the polite word

at an open door. Constancy enough,
for me, in her unvarying naked flesh,

those eyes whose level, blinkless glance
carried no spark of passion or intelligence.

How different now! A solitary image,
devoted, feeding children, showing age,

she questions me, her eyes aflame with needs
clarified at death-beds and on birth-beds.

And I, beside her sleep, and in her kitchen,
beloved, approved, indulged—a sombre man,

from phantasies of power, and sleights of will,
am brought at last to face the terrible

incarnation forced of things that are:
the Goddess as a chosen fellow creature.

Whom I must live with till my life is ended;
husband and master, mortal and afraid.

SAYING IT

QUESTIONS of tact are uppermost—
even when control appears to be lost;
to develop which, one cultivates silence
as well as words, weighing to the ounce
pauses long and short, awkward searchings,
and constructions that chase themselves in rings
till they peter away in utter defeat.
There may be a notable tact in that.
As in giving an embarrassing amount away,
in 'baring the soul' autobiographically,
in being tactless. What is demanded
is that the poet be openhanded
enough to allow his skill to grip
of all possible shapes the one shape
without which the poem would not be there—
chunky or clinking—fleshed from empty air.
It is like a good marriage: the man will know
the true wifely agreement from the say-so.
At times he will sulk, or shout, or practice disgust:
whichever seems to offer the most
likelihood of the hoped-for answer
to the non-questions it is impossible to ask her.
The tact is the keeping of a balance—
if that is what ensures, always, another chance.
Discounting nothing—kitchen trivia, boredom,
and the dreams of escape that make a home.

CAVALRY SKETCHES

B.A.O.R. 1948–1950

Baker, Abel, Oboe, Roger,
two sweltering summers, one iron winter
I dangled where your unmotherly breasts
spilled fifty per cent-plus rations! American
tinned bacon, Australian fruit cake, thievings
from orchards and hencoops, and duty-free
fags and tobacco. I failed exams,
grew ridged with muscle, and wrote poems
as others masturbated, able
to fold away only for some future self
the gutted cities, death-camps,
human stud farms, and monstrous statuary
of a Master Race which smilingly deferred
to justice, plebiscites, and spendthrift soldiers.

*   *   *

At Vogelsang there were little lakes
bright as the eyes in poems of women,
and Yeats and De La Mare were one
to me in those Shakespeare-and-Eliot days.
Sprawled on the head of the bullet-pocked Titan
that stood with flambeau raised and mighty
balls bare to Europe's winds,
you could see into Belgium, almost, across
the curly headed hills with their orbs
of azure water, the shattered huts
of the camp for Jewish Women, and
the rusting hulks of A.F.V.'s.
There were some famous victories
in those parts. I studied my precious poems.

*   *   *

S.S.M. Gower

Some joker called him 'Gypo', and it stuck
until he came to like it. Hook
of a nose, swarthy skin, eyes
that couldn't be fathomed. It was a good
name: he seemed to possess the power
of bilocation when double trouble
came. Straight from a hole in the road
into the army in '28,
he had fucked and blinded his trade across
half the Empire; the killed, the time-served,
and the bought-out wheeling and stamping perfectly,
still, on the great square of his mind.

To which we shuffled, late and awkward
additions to the dark trust he held.

* * *

Before first light we were up and gone
from the forest's edge, flinging lopped pine
branches from hulls and guns to the roar
of warming engines, and—while the thick
cow-high mist still hung like the trick
of a night-magician—(our drivers blind)
were clanking at top speed down unseen
lanes, our skulls full of the 'B' set's din.

Hot, futile days, and foolish battles—
blank against blank on the brain's gong;
now all's confused but the dappled road
where I craned to embrace a boughful of apples
as we crashed beneath, and hugged and hung
to fill the tank with the drumming load.

* * *

THE bleached heath was yielding up
the last of its colours. Waves of heat
buckled the low hills on the horizon;
near trees shivered like shaken stage flats.
We lazed beside our broken track
in the hull's hot shade. She tilted, settling
into the soft earth. The sky,
a ballooning blue all day, turned green,
a dusky green at evening. Then
we saw him coming—out of the silence
where blanks had been banging—
like a mirage, wobbling to solidity.
'The war's over!' he was whooping, his eyes
expressionless as his two brass pips.

*   *   *

In England yawning politicians
watched their friends and enemies carried
into the House; the radio said so,
but mostly the barracks blared with A.F.N.'s
bebop and Evangelism. The Russians
had closed Berlin. My roommate worried
himself silly after a film on V.D.—
disinfected his fraulein from head to toe
with Dettol. I was reading Eliot,
'the only poet'—even against the headphones'
shrieking voices as I crouched in a swaying turret,
while high in the open hatch's square of blue
flew the expedient planes of mercy
towards the divided, beleaguered city.

*   *   *

The six-hundred-horse-power Rolls Royce Meteor engine
could drive that bulk along good roads
at twenty-one miles an hour. Governed down
from its aero intention, it emitted clouds
of oily smoke when ticking-over, frustrating
camouflage behind buildings, or in thick woods
at five miles distance. The General's frown
(modelled on Rommel's) nearly knocked his binos
out of his hands; he shouted down the mike:
'For God's sake, John, get rid of that bloody smoke'—
as though it could be helped. The Colonel knew
he knew it couldn't, but made polite 'Wilco's',
and gave us all a lecture on concealment,
and the Regiment's proud record at Waterloo.

* * *

Sarg'

THE whiskey-tears were flowing again
for your downy comrades killed in the war.
You wept that you were to blame for
the deaths of many, and perhaps it was true;
earlier that day you had shown
spectacular cowardice, leaping from
our tank as it rolled like a bad dream
backwards down the hill, your crew
abandoned to an out-of-control
careering, thunderous coffin of metal.

You wiped your eyes in the gathering dark,
and ordered me to drink. The bivouack
was fugged with your shame. Later on
you tried to kiss me, but I was having none.

* * *

That summer we manouvered with the Yanks'
'Hell on Wheels' division—men and tanks
decorated bizarrely, as though Walt Disney
had advised on styling. Even our weird O.C.
with his greyhounds in the jeep, and his Turkish pistol,
thought them 'a bit much'. Swanning busily
about, we tried to find marshes for our Centurions
to sink in, while the nit-witted officers bit
their nails with battle-nerves, whispering 'Blueland must win'.
Sandhurst swelling the ranks of the Labour Party . . .
In the Camp Cinema, the Colonel announced war
in Korea. He looked drawn and thin
with suppressed excitement. Later there was a near-riot
when he announced an increase in the price of beer.

* * *

Arfer

ONTO his bed straight from the tankpark
in grease-stiff denims, he'd loll till dark
fingering himself beneath a picture
of an open-lipped big-breasted filmstar,
or else lie singing his mother's praises
as he scoffed her weekly parcel of pastries,
cakes, and sweets. His lumbering thoughts,
freed of immediate appetites,
sniffed round me at my *Four Quartets*;
vaguely perturbed at living with secrets
he wasn't in on. One bored night
he asked me to read 'some of that shit'
aloud. I started 'Burnt Norton',
but he was away with another hard-on.

* * *

16

Excused duties, hanging about for a week
after the trucks had left for the firing-range
with their yelling, healthy loads, I wandered the strange,
anonymous camp, where nobody stayed long.
The Guardhouse stones were unpainted, the windows broken.
Myself, a Torn Tendon, a buckshee clerk,
and a no-good cook were all that was left.
I twitched in the sun dreaming of newsreels: Belsen
was a mile past the pretty village. The Torn Tendon
decided to come, too, his black market Voigtlander
swinging sportily from his good shoulder.
But there wasn't a lot to see; in three years
they'd neatened and sweetened it beyond reason.
We snapped each other brooding as souvenirs.

FLIGHTS

As a child I was fortunate
in having the gift of flight.
Many familiar streets and bodies
I was able to view from eight feet
above ground level; many conversations
and quarrels I observed secretly
(being invisible).
I did not think it unusual.

Youth crippled the gift somewhat.
Only on certain nights
in cold, unpleasant dreams,
housebound and lapped by evil
airs and murmerings, did I float
like a grotesque balloon
over snoring sleepers,
and down draughty, threadbare stairs.

By eighteen I could not rise at all,
but—as though in compensation—
dead relatives, and earlier
occupants of the house
began to make themselves known to me.
The unloved—an asthmatic aunt,
two weeping second cousins,
a bearded suicide, and a baby

that choked on a boiled sweet—
all made importunate demands
I lacked the experience to
satisfy, or even to understand.
When I started writing poems
they stopped visiting me,

except for Uncle Harry
who insisted that he was my guide,

and under this pretext
succeeded in writing the memoirs
he had been revolving in his head
for twenty-five years
in the County Mental Hospital.
He was a man with eyes
like the winter sun's reflection
in two dust-laden windows;

I was glad to see him gone.
In mid-life I neither fly
nor receive the frustrated dead.
The days are women's baking smells,
and the demanding cries of children.
The nights, when they are broken,
are broken by flesh, and the sleepy moans
of my children learning to master flight.

DRUID'S CIRCLE

THE few squat leaning rocks in a loose ring
are a disappointment to all that climb
the mountain track to see them. They are nothing
like Auschwitz, Belsen, or Buchenwald. No crime

against humanity lingers in the air
of this place. The so-called 'Sacrificial
Stone' is a boring flat expanse, bare
of any hint of blood. It doesn't look especial

in the least—except for the roughly scratched
initials: a confused palimpsest
of clumsy letters cross-hatched
on its surface. To most people the trip's a waste

of time, and, if the women shudder,
the men light pipes, the children fret,
it is the wild-eyed ba-ba and scatter
of all that moving mutton, the sight

of so much horizon, and the air,
appalling in its emptiness,
that makes them loath to explore further,
and sends them townwards, laughing with distress.

ON THE CAMPUS

AMONG the frozen tarpaulins and the heaps
of sand and gravel, a fire leaps
at the low grey sky. They are burning the waste
of demolition. I feel myself becoming a ghost.

Here the narrow houses stood back to back.
All flattened; only a builder's shack
and gaslamps set as though by rule
across an emptiness act as a transient memorial.

Soon concrete and glass, with emerald lawns between,
will embody a multimillion-pound scheme;
an international centre of learning,
where I stumbled from wrong to right to wrong

for half a lifetime. There will not be a trace
of the district in which I sought a face
and found a poet's mask, amazed.
No poems but poems to be analysed.

I shiver, and it is not the frost, or the fog
come in from the suburbs. Cold epilogue
to a talent tied too closely to place,
and perished with it? No, I am glad of the release.

A faceless giant is walking on the grave
of someone ugly I grew to love.

A tractor is churning ice to mud;
erectors are bolting girders overhead.

APPROACHING BOLTON

BETWEEN the bridge and Moses Gate
close herbage blurs, we are flat out—

right on the governors. I imagine
something coming down on the same line.

Not really. For me, the leisurely bath
spoilt by the phone that stammers death,

the walk through trees to the cleaned-up site
of the gas chambers, the newsreel shot

of thousands of nameless bodies piled—
flesh burned away or disembowelled—

into mass graves somewhere else.
The stunned survivor's sense of guilt.

*

It is just an ordinary Tuesday
in mid-life; the same old journey

to earn my money, and back again
this evening on the stopping train.

Away to the left the town's sewage
settles through umpteen kinds of sludge

into a highly valued fertilizer,
and water that is officially pure.

*

Some have killed themselves, or gone mad
wearing the age's evil like a hood

they could not budge. The lucky man
staggers beneath his obscene burden

of luck, yet—sickened by common sense—
is glad of his life in a quiet province,

teaches his little children kerb-drill
although his nightmares are terrible.

*

Away to the right houses are going up
on the eminence of a filled-in tip.

The train stops at the scheduled platform,
I walk into town again without harm.

ABOVE PENMAENMAWR

THE upland farmers have all gone;
the lane they laid twists without purpose,
visiting broken gates and overgrown
gardens, to end in clumps of gorse.

Their unroofed houses, and fallen barns,
rich in nettles, lie dead in hiding
from the wind that howls off Talyfan's
saw-tooth ridge; their walls divide

bracken from bracken; their little church
of bare rock has outlasted use:
hikers' signatures in the porch,
'Keys obtainable at the Guesthouse'.

Yet, not to sentimentalize,
their faces turned from drudgery
when the chance showed itself. There is
hardly a sign of the husbandry

of even the last to leave—so slight
was their acceptance by the land.
They left for the seaside towns, to get
easier jobs, and cash in hand.

Five miles of uplands, and beyond—
a thousand feet below—the coast,
its bright lights twinkling; freezing wind
dragging the cloud down like a frost

from Talyfan. Alone upon
these darkening, silent heights, my fears
stay stubbornly with the farmers, gone
after six hundred thankless years.

ON THE CLIFF

BETWEEN the scented soap works
and cloud-capped cooling towers,
I walked one summer evening
swishing the soot-stained flowers.

Below, the black river
snaked around the racecourse,
drudging to distant sea
the dregs of commerce,

and huge across my vision
under the streaky sky
from Chapel Reach to Pomona Dock
the changing city lay,

swarming invisibly
with its intricate, restless hordes
of common humanity—
the keepers of the Word.

All I have accepted
to exercise heart and wit:
the unpredictable home
of the ever-unlikely poet.

There on the shifting cliff
where nothing built will stand—
local eruption of a fault
that runs across England—

I watched the lights come on,
and listened to a lover
coaxing a silent girl
under near cover,

25

and farther off the yells
of children at some chase;
voices much like my own—
the accent of the place.

The accent of the place!
My claim to a shared load
of general circumstance
with the hidden multitude.

Yet strange despite the wish,
because my chosen task
was the making of poems,
I shivered in the dusk,

aware that my shining city
did not care one jot
for me as its celebrant,
or whether I wrote or not.

I might have been unborn,
or else long dead,
but before I reached my home
I had perfected

the sociable, lonely poet,
a rueful one-man sect,
in an ignorant, ugly city—
his God-given subject.

CONSIDERING JUNK

It lies there, vivid in its dereliction,
among fine ashes from combustion stoves,
drippings of tinned tomatoes
that smelled peculiar, soiled disposable
nappies, and other household grot.

Having exhausted, or frustrated, expectation,
it emanates a certain smugness—
if you are of such a mind to think so.

A painter might take away the slither
of red polythene down a scorched bucket
into the crumbly texture of old flock
beneath: a sculptor—to the point of plundering—
broken bannister-ends like totems
to an ultimate, perfect, mass beyond masses.

You may look at it in different ways . . .

There are, for instance, certainly, numerous
homilies here for the religious man
with a touch of the poet.
                              As for the poet
himself; in this rigorous age he is wary of metaphor,
far more of symbol, and if he is the householder
(as I am) whose annual clear-out
has overflowed dustbin, grocery-boxes,
and mildewed, split trunk, onto
the garden path, his dreams alone are likely
to dwell on things he threw away.
                              Cumbersome, brokendown
junk talking all night with the eloquence of poems.

MY SISTER'S PAPERS

HER passport lies before me, open
at 'that atrocious photograph'.
It should be surrendered now she is dead.
But something makes me keep it; perhaps
I hope to see her face as she
saw it. To me the photograph
is a good likeness: cruel lips,
a gaze keen for fresh prey,
an arrogant smile. A good likeness
of her face at twenty, when last my sight
accepted her true image. Some
need of the heart cherishes wounds;
I would not see the changing woman
who visited home with smiles and presents.
She was still a selfish bitch, tolerated
for my mother's sake. What foolishness—
to make her pay for hurting me
by remaining the youth she hurt! Now
I study this recent photograph,
learning to hate it as she hated it.

THE GLOBE INN

I THINK of Dolly, last one at the feast:
picker of scraps from a bony carcase.
Three hundred years declined to this—
tradition living on as a deformed ghost
in the mind of an idiot.
                    The almost human
face drifting about the house,
mottled and round like the moon's face,
or bent over boiling chutney, through steam looming,
returns as an image overlaying the sign
of the globe from which continents had faded.
Sister, no more than a business head—
as alien as her long negotiation
to sell the place to a big brewery. The Severn
at the door, the water meadows,
the cathedral rising clear of the shadows
of Gloucester's ancient roofs—'a rural heaven
whose profits could be doubled if modernized'.

But Dolly with her fifteen tin
'wedding rings', her 'marriages' to fishermen,
and mongoloid smile, had nicknames for bird, beast,
and flower, saw the scattered family dying
in England's dirty cities.
                       'Flo
fell in the kitchen dead, I saw
while I was asleep.'
                   'Sarah is sick and going
to die, I spoke to her yesterday.'
                     'Uncle Jack
has gone to Heaven.'
                  Already the car-
trade gave the best returns. Sister
haggled about Goodwill with a man in black—

the brewery's representative—but died before
she could clinch the deal. Dolly saw
that coming, too, and whimpered in fear,
dreaming beside her glass beads and her teddy bear.

They put her in a Home. Sister willed
the Globe to the friend she'd not quite wed
because of Dolly: good, faithful, Jud
who'd helped in the bar for years. He sold
as quickly as he could. Dolly fell down
a flight of stairs and broke her neck;
the Matron stated she had been homesick.

My mother said: 'Well, that's the old place gone,
your grandma would have wept; she always thought
it was ours by rights.' And then: 'Poor Dolly.
I remember her as a child: poor Dolly.'

The end of a history; our last connection cut
with three hundred years of England. Never again
would Sister send us 'conscience money',
boxes of elvers—wet spaghetti
we tipped down the whiter pan and pulled the chain.

THE GAMEKEEPER'S DOTAGE

WHEN he was eighty-two they opened
the first of the Supermarkets
on the main road. I don't think
he even noticed the mighty pyramids
of tins and washing-up liquid
at cut prices piled in the window—
although one Sunday morning
he caught in bare hands
the panful of boiling peas
that tipped from his black hob.
The house was silent and dirty;
it stank as if death were there already;
you couldn't be sure in rooms
where you peered as though through water
that hadn't been changed for years.
Of course, you never stayed long, (the stench,
the dinginess, the look that showed—
again—he didn't know who you were)
but let him for his pride's sake brew
a pot of tea, and mumble for awhile
among his towering memories, which,
towards the end came down to one.

It was troubling to visit him by then;
to step from the main road's redevelopment,
the loaded shopping-bags, the lines
of shining cars, into that hush
where over and over he lifted arms
like trembling sticks, pulled the trigger,
and killed it for the Duke—the last
stag on the great estate
that has been a public park for fifty years.

KON IN SPRINGTIME

THE Russian landlord who lets next door's
once carefully cared-for rooms to any-
body, is angry about the money
that's gone from his desk. He doesn't mind whores,
or coloured students, or jailbirds,
or kids. He trails to the 'bins in a tatty
dressing-gown; up at seven-thirty,
shaking his aristocratic head

at the evil in men. I like sharing
the area with him; revolutions,
pogroms, years in a concentration
camp, haven't made him despair
of human nature. He won't call the police
(he never does), or tell the suspect
to get his paper-baggage packed—
and he isn't liberal-minded. He'll curse

rotten the dirty bastard who
robbed him, and make life unpleasant,
deliberately, for all his tenants
for at least a day, and perhaps two.
But can't for long not carry his years
gaily: the bow-tie, and the collar
of astrakhan are popular
sights in every local bar,

and at sixty-three, it's said, he still
has charm to enjoy the guarded virtue
of good wives, who open their legs to
nothing else that isn't legal.
May I survive a barbarous age
as well! Muttering and miming punches,
under a clear blue sky he crunches

back to the door across the spillage
of cinders from his pail. I watch
from the kitchen table, where I've sat
all night, struggling to be a poet
in mid-journey at masterful stretch
among the rich imperatives
of family life. The Russian pauses,
staring at me, as though my house is
haunted, reluctant to believe

I'm up at such an hour. He comes
worriedly to my window, certain
I must be awake because of children:
'Is it bad-sick—your little ones?'
he asks. I reassure him, they
vomited, but are asleep again.
He beams, who has never heard of Pushkin,
and says 'It will be a lovely day.'

THE BAT, THE RAT, THE STENCH,
THE LOCKED-OUT GOD

I

In a short dark passage
where the sitting room gave onto the kitchen
something was alive
and had been invisibly alive since the house was built.
It never declared itself
and he was unable to make up his mind
whether it was good or evil.

However, for purposes of self-defence,
he considered it evil.

When he journeyed
from one room to another
he hurried past the shadows
where its home was.

When he went to bed
alone in the house,
he folded his socks in the one appropriate way
and read precisely the fifteen pages of his library book.

If anyone had asked him
he would have laughed ridicule on them.

Sometimes he imagined it as a giant bat

an upside-down rat's face near the picture rail.

Sometimes he imagined it as a stench
concentrated over long years of self-regard
into a heavy squat shape, pulsing.

Sometimes he imagined it as rather like
'The Light of the World'
grown malevolent-eyed in the shine of the lantern.

II

BOYHOOD twitched to a kind of end.
He stopped worrying about it
and its most sinister aspect—its refusal to do
anything;
to engage in any demonstration of its existence
or of his existence.

No longer was he wrenched from sleep
into the dumb black
staring.
And what didn't or wasn't didn't or wasn't
for good reason.
Like a woman
or the plump presence of oranges
or international affairs
or clothes drying on a rack
or seats at the cinema.

III

HE married, and thought about buying a house.
He had forgotten it,
as though he had never had a childhood,
but some instinct told him
that houses with passages
and dark corners were no good.

He thought he had read the information in a magazine.

The house he chose was designed rationally.
The kitchen had a glass wall

35

and a serving hatch.
The scientifically placed lighting
banished shadows.

IV

By forty he was highly regarded in his profession,
and had accepted responsibility
for the world he lived in.

He tended mass graves,
was affected by Television Personalities,
waited patiently, alone in his six-seater car, at rush hour,
took packaged holidays in places off the beaten track,
studied close-ups of the moon's far side,
and gave to help peasants he need never see die.

V

One night he dreamed it came back out of nowhere
to bite his balls off.
But it was not a bat, or a rat,
or a stench grown solid,
or a locked-out God.

It was just a box, lopsided as if it were starting to melt.
It had hinged lids at one end
on which were painted jaws which moved feebly, creaking.
When he gave it a smack it rattled inside,
emitted a twang like a spring uncoiling,
the jaws stopped opening and closing
and it rolled slowly away.

He realized that had he not forgotten it
for the best part of a lifetime
he would have been tormented by fear
of this innocuous thing

36

lurking in the shadows of
his wife's groin,
his children's eyes,
his assistant's questions,
his enemy's plans,
his doctor's assurances.

He realized that it was nothing more than a foolish toy.

VI

THE man he was thought the thoughts he thought.

TWELVE SECRET POEMS

I

A GATHERING might begin it, or serve as spur,
so might the chosen cell.
Foreseen: micrometrically worked in steel
it might appear,
a repellant no-way-in sphere;
possibly, stood in a dark doorway,
a grubby unwanted visitor

ill-clad for that, or any other, feast.
There are no precedents;
nothing in books, in memories of events,
to help construct
the like of it. Personally lacked
(except in dream, where even Easter
craves your own face), its past

appearances taunt now with joyous Amens.
No formula suffices;
nor will the stars jag from their courses,
respectively,
to make it, to prove its cosmic urgency.
At best a kind of still dancing
augurs presence; at worst, irons

burst from exploding lungs, death lets in light.
These wonders could be truth:
it might resemble you, be you; a path
taken, a rag
richly embroidered, a belly big
before childbirth, my hand writing,
a star, a sphere, a beggar, manifold sight.

II

HERE are the forgotten dead
who sit about on unidentified beaches
under enormous hats,
or look back, smiling,
from actions they are about to take.
Fragments of a completeness
that may in no way be changed.

Yet vaguely, surely,
modifying the latest will
as it falters from love,
or manoeuvres weightlessly
above the coloured ball of earth.

III

DULL headaches on dark afternoons
suggest the suburbs of Hell;
a city one's friends will never drive across,
where the telephone never rings.

There was something to think about . . .
a claim on insurance . . . China . . .
the rationalization of the Aircraft Industry . . .
or was it new shoes for the children?

One could pull down reputations
in the mind: Tiepolo tumbling;
Marvell going over with a shriek.
Bach and Shakespeare are not safe on a day like this.

Remember different women: those variations
on the one smell. Perhaps in Heaven
you could stay in bed forever
and never sicken of flesh or sleep.

Now the rain is beginning . . . orange lights
are flickering to life on the main road.
When the hidden sun sets so early
the appetite for subtleties is blunted, or disappears;

the mind hankers after final judgements,
crosses and ticks . . . ticks and crosses.
But soon the usual visitors will arrive,
those you dislike, you think, but can't be sure.

IV

ONE does not ask for
or want them: nightmare
black lakes' death you hang
between on mossed plank
from a glance inside
the loud cistern's crude
box or the martyr's
last moment terrors
in a finger's dull
pain on a pipeful
of hot tobacco—
rather would you be
dignified and moved
to poems by braved
extremes of the world's
cruelty; but skilled
at cashing-in on
inferred occasion
this is what you must
suffer in your most
comfortable home:
never to be dumb.

V

STRIDING its den, cold cage of winter,
the tiger-eye snarls for forests,
meat that's yet throbbing beneath hair.

Nothing's about but what looks in,
sniggers, and sucks back its breath's bloom;
the sky is probably all of scratched wood.

At night there are lights and men shouting,
near and hidden; music, machines,
and the screams of women searching for secret pain,

skirts whipped from their thighs by wind.

The tiger-eye searches the darkness,
but cannot find its two legs, its sweet voice.

VI

THERE is a war going on.
Outside, gangs of youths
are looking for things to kill;
petals are smouldering in the garden.

You have been reading a book
for thirty-six years: a book about nothing:
you have four fine children
and a responsible position.

The old folk do not care about history,
but there is entertainment value
in world disorder;
they are glued to their television sets.

It is not as you thought it would be;
last week you scooped the pools,
and you are better looking
than you were as a young man.

The war is worrying, but you stay home;
your larder will outlast the worst,
your long poem only needs polishing,
there are no more best friends left to die.

VII

SEEING a face open
eyes of gun grey
hinting what then

A steady quick run
away away away
seeing a face open

in laughter boredom pain
you might begin to say
hinting what then

Certainly a woman
breasts hips sway
seeing a face open

And all in bright sun
on a confused day
hinting what then

Sometimes you can't begin
the mind's too slow
seeing a face open
hinting what then

VIII

Do not believe it dies, though many signs
suggest that worse is getting worse.
Grids are swallowing more of it every day,
already its strong voice tends towards silence.

Of course you are differently stripped in bed
from last year's nakedness; there are fewer
friends at your door; certain woods warp.
The sodium lamps are gobbling up the daylight.

Almost as if it had a hidden grudge
against your senses, it is turning away
from nostrils, ears, eyes, fingers; even your tongue
has hardly a morsel left, makes words that sound dead.

Study it as it goes! That smokiness in the trees,
that careless woman brooding about a lock
on the front door, might tell you what it's like—
whether drugs or agony best suit its style.

For you, the Spring shall need it as a memory,
no more. You will be here, polishing plates and verses,
and maybe forever. Wanting a last breath,
a wife with wrinkled breasts, children who outlive you.

IX

FROM wrestling all night
with the Prince of Darkness,
to wake with the stink
upon your hands in a room
bright with August sunlight.

The underbelly of beauty
crawls with worse than lice.

I revive by touching
the hair of infants.

X

I BEGIN by being watched;
(do not try to reward me,
I cannot be rewarded).
Everyone else in the house is asleep

It is the bleak dead,
the battle-stained dead
lapping the black blood;
what can I say at the world's end?

Tick tock tick tock the ancient clock,
I am Alpha, I am Omega;
a child cries in its sleep.
The way is plain and chills the heart.

Who placed this strange chair
in the corner of my eye?
Who found me here this night
and all the silent nights without number?

If I am being watched
I am being watched
to no help and no hindrance;
the reward of speech is speech.

You with the broken neck, lie quiet;
old blind sage be still.
The clock whirrs and strikes the hour.
My children will wake happy.

XI

ONE might go round and round for ever,
or dissolve into
the grease on dining plates.

One might become one's thoughts
about oneself, or polish taps
day after day until
one's image in the convex chrome
sufficed. One might go round and round
the endless streets, or wander
where all cairns look alike
and the occasional glint
of distant sea means nothing
but shining water.
                    Women, words,
what is expected of you.

One might go round and round for ever.

XII

We have covered the mirrors and Master's face,
the old house settles to silence,
each of us in his proper place.

Nothing disturbs the hanging lace,
the air is motionless and dense;
we have covered the mirrors and Master's face.

Nobody weeps, nobody prays,
yet who would doubt our reverence,
each of us in his proper place?

The last and finest of the race,
nobly he endured his going hence;
we have covered the mirrors and Master's face

Now time is meaningless, and space;
we hope for nothing from events,
each of us in his proper place.

Approaching the door, the measured pace
of heartless, legal ignorance.
We have covered the mirrors and Master's face,
each of us in his proper place.